Bite Sized Books publishing
https://bitesizedbook.com

Curated by J Bylund
https://jesperbylund.com

ISBN: 978-91-519-3576-8

BY J BYLUND

On the 31st of May 2018, Naval posted what is now considered to be classic advice on how to get rich on Twitter.

His practical advice and relatable goals made Naval famous over night among entrepreneurs and people all over the world who were looking for economic freedom.

I was personally in a slump in my life when Naval's ideas reached me. They spurred me to retake agency over my own life, and in the less than two years since I've made more progress than in the previous decade.

This is why I want to spread Naval's ideas. This book is my way to help other discover these powerful tools, and hopefully help them as they have helped me.

Practically the book is a collection of both the original advice from Twitter as well as the follow ups by Naval across podcasts and interviews the following year.

   – J

   Naval himself has had nothing to do with this project and probably does not even know this book exists. This is merely a curated collection of his timeless advice.

Introduction   2

1. Seek wealth, not money or status   6

2. Ethical wealth creation is possible   12

3. Ignore people playing status games   16

4. Renting out your time   17

5. At scale   23

6. Play long term games   27

7. Possibility space   34

8. Compound interest   40

9. Business partners   41

10. Don't partner with cynics and pessimists   47

11. Learn to sell   53

12. Arm yourself with specific knowledge   59

13. What specific knowledge is   66

14. Where specific knowledge is found   67

15. Building specific knowledge   68

16. Where specific knowledge is taught   69

17. Specific knowledge cannot be automated   70

18. Embrace accountability   76

19. Singular, public, and risky brands   82

20. Archimedes   83

21. Fortunes require leverage 89

22. Capital means money 90

23. Labor 91

24. Permissioned leverage 92

25. Permissionless leverage 93

26. An army of robots 99

27. If you can't, you can 100

28. Judgement 101

29. Experience 109

30. No skill called "business" 110

31. What to study 116

32. Learning faster 117

33. Too busy to "do coffee" 118

34. Personal hourly rate 123

35. Work as hard as you can 128

36. Become the best in the world 134

37. There are no get rich quick schemes 137

38. Apply specific knowledge 143

39. What you were seeking in the first place 148

How to Get Rich (without getting lucky) 153

1

"Seek wealth, not money or status. Wealth is having assets that earn while you sleep. Money is how we transfer time and wealth. Status is your place in the social hierarchy."

Wealth is assets that earn while you sleep

Nivi: What's the difference between wealth, money, and status?

Naval: Wealth is the thing that you want. Wealth is assets that earn while you sleep. Wealth is the factory, the robots, that's cranking out things. Wealth is the computer program that's running at night, that's serving other customers. Wealth is even money in the bank that is being reinvested into other assets, and into other businesses.

Even a house can be a form of wealth because you can rent it out, although that's probably a lower use of productivity of land than doing some commercial enterprise.

So, my definition of wealth is much more businesses and assets that can earn while you sleep.

Wealth buys your freedom

The reason you want wealth is because it buys you your freedom. So, you don't have to wear a tie like a collar around your neck. So, you don't have to wake up at 7:00 AM, and rush to work, and sit in commute traffic. So, you don't have to waste away your entire life grinding all your productive hours away into a soulless job that doesn't fulfill you.

So, the purpose of wealth is freedom. It's nothing more than that. It's not to buy fur coats, or drive Ferraris, or sail yachts, or jet around the world in your Gulfstream. That stuff gets really boring and really stupid, really fast. It's really so that you are your own sovereign individual.

You're not going to get that unless you really want it. The entire world wants it and the entire world is working hard at it.

To some extent it is competitive. It's a positive sum game, but there are competitive elements to it. Because there's a finite amount of resources right now in society. To get the resources to do what you want, you have to stand out.

Money is how we transfer wealth

Money is how we transfer wealth. Money is social credits. It is the ability to have credits and debits of other people's time.

If I do my job right, if I create value for society, society says, "Oh, thank you. We owe you something in the future for the work that you did in the past. Here's a little IOU. Let's call that money."

That money gets debased because people steal the IOUs. The government prints extra IOUs. People renege on their IOUs. But money is trying to be a reliable IOU from society that you are owed something for something you, or someone who gave you the money, did in the past.

We can transfer these IOUs around. So, money is how we transfer wealth.

Status is your rank in the social hierarchy

There are fundamentally two huge games in life that people play. One is the money game. Because money is not going to solve all of your problems, but it's going to solve all of your money problems. I think people know that. They realize that, so they want to make money.

But at the same time, many of them deep down believe that they can't make it. They don't want any wealth creation to happen. So, they virtue signal by attacking the whole enterprise by saying, "Well, making money is evil. You shouldn't do it."

But they're actually playing the other game, which is the status game. They're trying to be high status in the eyes of other people watching by saying, "Well, I don't need money. We don't want money."

Status is your ranking in the social hierarchy.

Wealth is not a zero-sum game. Everybody in the world can have a house. Because you have a house doesn't take away from my ability to have a house. If anything, the more houses that are built, the easier it becomes to build houses, the more we know about building houses, and the more people that can have houses.

Wealth is a very positive sum game. We create things together. We're starting this endeavor to create this piece of art that explains what we're doing. At the end of it, something brand new will be created. It's a positive sum game.

Status is a very old game

Status, on the other hand, is a zero-sum game. It's a very old game. We've been playing it since monkey tribes. It's hierarchical. Who's number one? Who's number two? Who's number three? And for number three to move to number two, number two has to move out of that slot. So, status is a zero-sum game.

Politics is an example of a status game. Even sports is an example of a status game. To be the winner, there must be a loser. I don't fundamentally love status games. They play an important role in our society, so we can figure out who's in charge. But fundamentally, you play them because they're a necessary evil.

On an evolutionary basis, if you go back thousands of years, status is a much better predictor of survival than wealth is. You couldn't have wealth before the farming age because you couldn't store things. Hunter-gatherers carried everything on their backs.

So, hunter-gatherers lived in entirely status based societies. Farmers started going to wealth-based societies. And the modern industrial economies are much more heavily wealth-based societies.

People creating wealth will always be attacked by people playing status games

There's always a subtle competition going on between status and wealth. For example, when journalists attack rich people, or attack the technology industry, they're really bidding for status. They're saying, "No, the people are more important. And I, the journalist, represent the people, and therefore I am more important."

The problem is that to win at a status game, you have to put somebody else down. That's why you should avoid status games in your life because they make you into an angry combative person. You're always fighting to put other people down, to put yourself and the people you like up.

Status games are always going to exist. There's no way around it, but realize that most of the time, when you're trying to create wealth, you're getting attacked by someone else, and they're trying to look like a goody-two shoes.

They're trying to up their own status at your expense. They're playing a different game. And it's a worse game. It's a zero-sum game, instead of a positive sum game.

2

"Understand that ethical wealth creation is possible. If you secretly despise wealth, it will elude you."

Ethical wealth creation makes abundance for the world

Naval: I think there is this notion that making money is evil, right? It's rooted all the way back down to "money is the root of all evil." People think that the bankers steal our money. It's somewhat true in that, in a lot of the world, there's a lot of theft going on all the time.

The history of the world, in some sense, is this predator/prey relationship between makers and takers. There are people who go out and create things, and build things, and work hard on things.

Then there are people who come along with a sword, or a gun, or taxes, or crony capitalism, or Communism, or what have you. There's all these different methods to steal.

Even in nature, there are more parasites than there are non-parasitical organisms. You have a ton of parasites in you, who are living off of you. The better ones are symbiotic, they're giving something back. But there are a lot that are just taking. That's the nature of how any complex system is built.

What I am focused on is true wealth creation. It's not about taking money. It's not about taking something from somebody else. It's from creating abundance.

Obviously, there isn't a finite number of jobs, or finite amount of wealth. Otherwise we would still be sitting around in caves, figuring out how to divide up pieces of fire wood, and the occasional dead deer.

Most of the wealth in civilization, in fact all of it, has been created. It got created from somewhere. It got created from people. It got created from technology. It got created from productivity. It got created from hard work. This idea that it's stolen is this horrible zero-sum game that people who are trying to gain status play.

Everyone can be rich

But the reality is everyone can be rich. We can see that by seeing, that in the First World, everyone is basically richer than almost anyone who was alive 200 years ago.

200 years ago nobody had antibiotics. Nobody had cars. Nobody had electricity. Nobody had the iPhone. All of these things are inventions that have made us wealthier as a species.

Today, I would rather be a poor person in a First World country, than be a rich person in Louis the XIV's France. I'd rather be a poor person today than aristocrat back then. That's because of wealth creation.

The engine of technology is science that is applied for the purpose of creating abundance. So, I think fundamentally everybody can be wealthy.

This thought experiment I want you to think through is imagine if everybody had the knowledge of a good software engineer and a good hardware engineer. If you could go out there, and you could build robots, and computers, and bridges, and program them. Let's say every human knew how to do that.

What do you think society would look like in 20 years? My guess is what would happen is we would build robots, machines, software and hardware to do everything. We would all be living in massive abundance.

We would essentially be retired, in the sense that none of us would have to work for any of the basics. We'd even have robotic nurses. We'd have machine driven hospitals. We'd have self-driving cars. We'd have farms that are 100% automated. We'd have clean energy.

At that point, we could use technology breakthroughs to get everything that we wanted. If anyone is still working at that point, they're working as a form of expressing their creativity. They're working because it's in them to contribute, and to build and design things.

I don't think capitalism is evil. Capitalism is actually good. It's just that it gets hijacked. It gets hijacked by improper pricing of externalities. It gets hijacked by improper yields, where you have corruption, or you have monopolies.

3

"Ignore people playing status games. They gain status by attacking people playing wealth creation games."

Discussed in <u>chapter 1</u>.

4

. . . .

"You're not going to get rich renting out your time. You must own equity - a piece of a business - to gain your financial freedom."

. . . .

You won't get rich renting out your time

Nivi: Next you go into more specific details on how you can actually get rich, and how you can't get rich. The first point was about how you're not going to get rich: "You are not going to get rich renting out your time. You must own equity, a piece of the business to gain your financial freedom."

Naval: This is probably one of the absolute most important points. People seem to think that you can create wealth, and make money through work. And it's probably not going to work. There are many reasons for that.

But the most basic is just that your inputs are very closely tied to your outputs. In almost any salaried job, even at one that's paying a lot per hour like a lawyer, or a doctor, you're still putting in the hours, and every hour you get paid.

So, what that means is when you're sleeping, you're not earning. When you're retired, you're not earning. When you're on vacation, you're not earning. And you can't earn non-linearly.

If you look at even doctors who get rich, like really rich, it's because they open a business. They open like a private practice. And that private practice builds a brand, and that brand attracts people. Or they build some kind of a medical device, or a procedure, or a process with an intellectual property.

So, essentially you're working for somebody else, and that person is taking on the risk, and has the accountability, and the intellectual property, and the brand. So, they're just not gonna pay you enough. They're gonna pay you the bare minimum that they have to, to get you to do their job. And that can be a high bare minimum, but it's still not gonna be true wealth where you're retired.

Renting out your time means you're essentially replaceable

And then finally you're actually just not even creating that much original for society. Like I said, this tweetstorm should have been called "How to Create Wealth." It's just "How to Get Rich" was a more catchy title. But you're not creating new things for society. You're just doing things over and over.

And you're essentially replaceable because you're now doing a set role. Most set roles can be taught. If they can be taught like in a school, then eventually you're gonna be competing with someone who's got more recent knowledge, who's been taught, and is coming in to replace you.

You're much more likely to be doing a job that can be eventually replaced by a robot, or by an AI. And it doesn't even have to be wholesale replaced over night. It can be replaced a little bit at a time. And that kind of eats into your wealth creation, and therefore your earning capability.

So, fundamentally your inputs are matched to your outputs. You are replaceable, and you're not being creative. I just don't think that, that is a way that you can truly make money.

You must own equity to gain your financial freedom

So everybody who really makes money at some point owns a piece of a product, or a business, or some kind of IP. That can be through stock options, so you can be working at a tech company. That's a fine way to start.

But usually the real wealth is created by starting your own companies, or by even investors. They're in an investment firm, and they're buying equity. These are much more the routes to wealth. It doesn't come through the hours.

You want a career where your inputs don't match your outputs

You really just want a job, or a career, or a profession where your input is don't match your outputs. If you look at modern society, again this is later in the tweetstorm. Businesses that have high creativity and high leverage tends to be ones where you could do an hour of work, and it can have a huge effect. Or you can do 1,000 hours of work, and it can have no effect.

For example, look at software engineering. One great engineer can for example create bitcoin, and create billions of dollars worth of value. And an engineer who is working on the wrong thing, or not quite as good, or just not as creative, or thoughtful, or whatever, can work for an entire a year, and every piece of code they ship ends up not getting used. Customers don't want it.

That is an example of a profession where the input and the outputs are highly disconnected. It's not based on the number of hours that you put in.

Whereas on the extreme other end, if you're a lumberjack, even the best lumberjack in the world, assuming you're not working with tools, so the inputs and outputs are clearly connected. You're just using an ax, or a saw. You know, the best lumberjack in the world may be like 3x better than one of the worst lumberjacks, right? It's not gonna be a gigantic difference.

So, you want to look for professions and careers where the inputs and outputs are highly disconnected. This is another way of saying that you want to look for things that are leveraged. And by leveraged I don't mean financial leveraged alone, like Wall Street uses, and that has a bad name. I'm just talking about tools. We're using tools.

Computer is a tool that software engineers use. If I'm a lumberjack with bulldozers, and automatic robot axes, and saws, I'm gonna be using tools, and have more leverage than someone who is just using his bare hands, and trying to rip the trees out by the roots.

Tools and leverage are what create this disconnection between inputs and outputs. Creativity, so the higher the creativity component of a profession, the more likely it is to have disconnected inputs and outputs.

So, I think that if you're looking at professions where your inputs and your outputs are highly connected, it's gonna very, very, hard to create wealth, and make wealth for yourself in that process.

5

. . . .

"You will get rich by giving society what it wants but does not yet know how to get. At scale. "

. . . .

Give society what it wants, but doesn't know how to get—at scale

Nivi: You're not gonna get rich renting out your time. But you say that, "you will get rich by giving society what it wants, but does not yet know how to get at scale."

Naval: That's right. So, essentially as we talked about before, money is IOUs from society saying, "You did something good in the past. Now here's something that we owe you for the future." And so society will pay you for creating things that it wants.

But society doesn't yet know how to create those things because if it did, they wouldn't need you. They would already be stamped out big time.

Almost everything that's in your house, in your workplace, and on the street used to be technology at one point in time. There was a time when oil was a technology, that made J.D. Rockefeller rich. There was a time when cars were technology, that made Henry Ford rich.

So, technology is just the set of things, as Alan Kay said, that don't quite work yet [correction: Danny Hillis]. Once something works, it's no longer technology. So, society always wants new things.

Figure out what product you can provide and then figure out how to scale it

And if you want to be wealthy, you want to figure out which one of those things you can provide for society, that it does not yet know how to get, but it will want, that's natural to you, and within your skillset, within your capabilities.

And then you have to figure out how to scale it. Because if you just build one of it, that's not enough. You've got to build thousands, or hundreds of thousands, or millions, or billions of them. So, everybody can have one.

Steve Jobs, and his team of course figured out that society would want smartphones. A computer in their pocket that had all the phone capability times 100, and be easy to use. So, they figured out how to build that, and then they figured out how to scale it.

And they figured out how to get one into every First World citizen's pocket, and eventually every Third World citizen too. And so because of that they're handsomely rewarded, and Apple is the most valuable company in the world.

Nivi: The way I tried to put it was that the entrepreneur's job is to try to bring the high end to the mass market.

Naval: It starts as high end. First it starts as an act of creativity. First you create it just because you want it. You want it, and you know how to build it, and you need it. And so you build it for yourself. Then you figure out how to get it to other people. And then for a little while rich people have it.

Like, for example rich people had chauffeurs, and then they had black town cars. And then Uber came along, and everyone's private driver is available to everybody. And now you can even see Uber pools that are replacing shuttle buses because it's more convenient. And then you get scooters, which are even further down market of that. So, you're right. It's about distributing what rich people used to have to everybody.

But the entrepreneur's job starts even before that, which is creation. Entrepreneurship is essentially an act of creating something new from scratch. Predicting that society will want it, and then figuring out how to scale it, and get it to everybody in a profitable way, in a self-sustaining way.

6

. . . .

"Pick an industry where you can play long term games with long term people."

. . . .

Nivi: Talk a little bit about what industries you should think about working in. What kind of job you should have? And who you might want to work with? So, you said, "One should pick an industry where you can play long-term games with long-term people." Why?

Naval: Yeah, this is an insight into what makes Silicon Valley work, and what makes high trust societies work. Essentially, all the benefits in life come from compound interests. Whether it's in relationships, or making money, or in learning.

So, compound interest is a marvelous force, where if you start out with 1x what you have, and then if you increase 20% a year for 30 years, it's not that you got 30 years times 20% added on. It was compounding, so it just grew, and grew, and grew until you suddenly got a massive amount of whatever it is. Whether it's goodwill, or love, or relationships, or money. So, I think compound interest is a very important force.

You have to be able to play a long-term game. And long-term games are good not just for compound interest, they're also good for trust. If you look at prisoner's dilemma type games, a solution to prisoner's dilemma is tit-for-tat, which is I'm just going do to you what you did last time to me, with some forgiveness in case there was a mistake made. But that only works in an iterated prisoner's dilemma, in another words if we play a game multiple times.

So, if you're in a situation, like for example you're in Silicon Valley, where people are doing business with each other, and they know each other, they trust each other. Then they do right by each other because they know this person will be around for the next game.

Now of course that doesn't always work because you can make so much money in one move in Silicon Valley, sometimes people betray each other because they're just like, "I'm going to get rich enough off this that I don't care." So, there can be exceptions to all these circumstances.

But essentially if you want to be successful, you have to work with other people. And you have to figure out who can you trust, and who can you trust over a long, long period of time, that you can just keep playing the game with them, so that compound interest, and high trust will make it easier to play the game, and will let you collect the major rewards, which are usually at the end of the cycle.

So, for example, Warren Buffett has done really well as an investor in the U.S. stock market, but the biggest reason he could do that was because the U.S. stock market has been stable, and around, and didn't get for example seized by the government during a bad administration. Or the U.S. didn't plunge into some war. The underlying platform didn't get destroyed. So, in his case, he was playing a longterm game. And the trust came from the U.S. stock market's stability.

When you switch industries, you're starting over from scratch

In Silicon Valley, the trust comes from the network of people in the small geographic area, that you figure out over time who you can work with, and who you can't.

If you keep switching locations, you keep switching groups… let's say you started out in the woodworking industry, and you built up a network there. And you're working hard, you're trying to build a product in the woodworking industry. And then suddenly another industry comes along that's adjacent but different, but you don't really know anybody in it, and you want to dive in, and make money there.

If you keep hopping from industry to … "No, actually I need to open a line of electric car stations for electric car refueling." That might make sense. That might be the best opportunity. But every time you reset, every time you wander out of where you built your network, you're going to be starting from scratch. You're not going to know who to trust. They're not going to know to trust you.

There are also industries in which people are transient by definition. They're always coming in and going out. Politics is an example of that, right? In politics new people are being elected. You see in politics that when you have a lot of old-timers, like the Senate, people who have been around for a long time, and they've been career politicians.

There's a lot of downside to career politicians like corruption. But an upside is they actually get deals done with each other because they know the other person is going to be in the same position ten years from now, and they're going to have to keep dealing with them, so they might as well learn how to cooperate.

Whereas every time you get a new incoming freshman class in the House of Representatives, which turns over every two years with a big wave election. Nothing gets done because of a lot fighting. "Because I just got here, I don't know you, I don't know if you're going to be around, why should I work with you rather than just try to do whatever I think is right?"

So, it's important to pick an industry where you can play long-term games, and with long-term people. So, those people have to signal that they're going to be around for a long time. That they're ethical. And their ethics are visible through their actions.

Long-term players make each other rich

Nivi: In a long-term game, it seems that everybody is making each other rich. And in a short-term game, it seems like everybody is making themselves rich.

Naval: I think that is a brilliant formulation. In a longterm game, it's positive sum. We're all baking the pie together. We're trying to make it as big as possible. And in a short term game, we're cutting up the pie.

Now this is not to excuse the socialists, right? The socialists are the people who are not involved in baking the pie, who show up at the end, and say, "I want a slice, or I want the whole pie." They show up with the guns.

But I think a good leader doesn't take credit. A good leader basically tries to inspire people, so the team gets the job done. And then things get divided up according to fairness, and who contributed how much, or as close to it as possible, and took a risk, as opposed to just whoever has the longest knife… the sharpest knife at the end.

Returns come from compound interest in iterated games

Nivi: So, these next two tweets are, "Play iterated games. All returns in life, whether in wealth, relationships, or knowledge come from compound interest."

Naval: When you have been doing business with somebody, you've been friends with somebody for ten years, twenty years, thirty years, it just gets better and better because you trust them so easily. The friction goes down, you can do bigger, and bigger things together.

For example, the simplest one is getting married to someone, and having kids, and raising children. That's compound interest, right? Investing in those relationships. Those relationships end up being invaluable compared to more casual relationships.

It's true in health and fitness. You know, the fitter you are, the easier it is to stay fit. Whereas the more you deteriorate your body, the harder it is to come back, and claw your way back to a baseline. It requires heroic acts.

Nivi: Regarding compound interest, I think I saw retweet something a while back. Maybe it was from Ed Latimore. It went something along the lines of, "Get some traction. Get purchase, and don't lose it" (correction: the tweet is by Michael, or @mmay3r on twitter). So, the idea was to gain some initial traction, and never fall back, just keep ratcheting up, and up.

Naval: I don't remember it exactly. But I think that was right. Yes, it was like, "Get traction, and don't let go." It was a good one, yes.

7

. . . .

"The Internet has massively broadened the possible space of careers. Most people haven't figured this out yet."

. . . .

The Internet has massively broadened the possible space of careers

Nivi: Let's look at this next tweet, which I thought was cryptic, and also super interesting, about the kind of job or career that you might have. You said, "The internet has massively broadened the possible space of careers. Most people haven't figured this out yet."

Naval: The fundamental property of the internet more than any other single thing is it connects every human to each other human on the planet. You can now reach everyone.

Whether it's by emailing them personally, whether it's by broadcasting to them on Twitter, whether it's by posting something on Facebook that they find, whether it's by putting up a website they come and access.

It connects everyone to everyone. So, the internet is an inter-networking tool. It connects everybody. That is its superpower. So, you want to use that.

What that helps you figure out is the internet means you can find your audience for your product, or your talent, and skill no matter how far away they are.

For example, Nenad, who is Illacertus, if you look at his videos pre-internet, how would he get the message out there? It would just be … what would he do? He would run around where he lives in his neighborhood showing it to people on a computer, or a screen? Or he would try to get it played at his local movie theater? It was impossible. It only works because he can put it on the internet.

And then how many people in the world are really interested in it? Or even in interested in what we're talking about are really gonna absorb it, right? It's gonna be a very small subset of humanity. The key is being able to reach them.

The Internet allows you to scale any niche obsession

So, what the internet does is allows any niche obsession, which could be just the weirdest thing. It could be like people who collect snakes, to like people who like to ride hot air balloons, to people who like to sail around the world by themselves, just one person on a craft, or someone who's obsessed with miniature cooking. Like, there's this whole Japanese miniature cooking phenomenon. Or there's a show about a woman who goes in people's houses, and tidies it up, right?

So, whatever niche obsession you have, the internet allows you to scale. Now that's not to say that what you build will be the next Facebook, or reach billions of users, but if you just want to reach 50,000 passionate people like you, there's an audience out there for you.

So the beauty of this is that we have 7 billion human beings on the planet. The combinatorics of human DNA are incredible. Everyone is completely different. You'll never meet any two people who are even vaguely similar to each other, that can substitute for each other.

It's not like you can say, "Well, Nivi, just left my life. So, I can have this other person come in, and he's just like Nivi. And I get the same feelings, and the same responses, and the same ideas." No. There are no substitutes for people. People are completely unique.

So, given that each person has different skillsets, different interests, different obsessions. And it's that diversity that becomes a creative superpower. So, each person can be creatively superb at their own unique thing.

But before that didn't matter. Because if you were living in a little fishing village in Italy, like your fishing village didn't necessarily need your completely unique skill, and you had to conform to just the few jobs that were available. But now today you can be completely unique.

You can go out on the internet, and you can find your audience. And you can build a business, and create a product, and build wealth, and make people happy just uniquely expressing yourself through the internet.

The space of careers has been so broadened. E-sports players, you know, people making millions of dollars playing Fortnite. People creating videos, and uploading them. YouTube broadcasters. Bloggers, podcasters. Joe Rogan, I read, true or false, I don't know, but I read that he's gonna make about $100 million a year on his podcast. And he's had 2 billion downloads.

Even PewDiePie… there's a hilarious tweet that I retweeted the other day. PewDiePie is the number one trusted name in news. This is a kid I think in Sweden, and he's got three times the distribution of the top cable news networks. Just on his news channel. It's not even on his entertainment channel.

Escape competition through authenticity

The internet enables any niche interest, as long as you're the best at it to scale out. And the great news is because every human is different, everyone is the best at something. Being themselves.

Another tweet I had that is worth kind of weaving in, but didn't go into this tweetstorm, was a very simple one. I like things when I can compress them down because they're easy to remember, and easy to hook onto. But that one was, "Escape competition through authenticity."

Basically, when you're competing with people it's because you're copying them. It's because you're trying to do the same thing. But every human is different. Don't copy.

I know we're mimetic creatures, and René Girard has a whole mimesis theory. But it's much easier than that. Don't imitate. Don't copy. Just do your own thing. No one can compete with you on being you. It's that simple.

And so the more authentic you are to who you are, and what you love to do, the less competition you're gonna have. So, you can escape competition through authenticity when you realize that no one can compete with you on being you. And normally that would have been useless advice pre-internet. Post-internet you can turn that into a career.

8

"Play iterated games. All the returns in life, whether in wealth, relationships, or knowledge, come from compound interest."

Discussed in <u>chapter 6</u>.

9

· ·

"Pick business partners with high intelligence, energy, and, above all, integrity."

· ·

Pick business partners with high intelligence, energy and integrity

Naval: In terms of picking people to work with, pick ones that have high intelligence, high energy, and high integrity, I find that's the three-part checklist that you cannot compromise on.

You need someone who is smart, or they'll head in the wrong direction. And you're not going to end up in the right place. You need someone high-energy because the world is full of smart, lazy people.

We all know people in our life who are really smart, but can't get out of bed, or lift a finger. And we also know people who are very high energy, but not that smart. So, they work hard, but they're sort of running in the wrong direction.

And smart is not a pejorative. It's not meant to say someone is smart, someone else is stupid. But it's more that everyone is smart at different things. So, depending on what you want to do well, you have to find someone who is smart at that thing.

And then energy, a lot of times people are unmotivated for a specific thing, but they're motivated for other things. So, for example, someone might be really unmotivated to go to a job, and sit in an office. But they might be really motivated to go paint, right?

Well, in that case they should be a painter. They should be putting art up on the internet. Trying to figure out how to build a career out of that, rather than wearing a collar around their neck, and going to a dreary job.

And then high integrity is the most important because otherwise if you've got the other two, what you have is you have a smart and hard working crook, who's eventually going to cheat you. So, you have to figure out if the person is high-integrity.

And as we talked about, the way you do that is through signals. And signals is what they do, not what they say. It's all the non-verbal stuff that they do when they think nobody is looking.

Motivation has to come intrinsically

Nivi: With respect to the energy, there was this interesting thing from Sam Altman a while back, where he was talking about delegation, and he was saying, "One of the important things for delegation is, delegate to people who are actually good at the thing that you want them to do."

It's the most obvious thing, but it seems like... you want to partner with people who are naturally going to do the things that you want them to do.

Naval: Yeah. I almost won't start a company, or hire a person, or work with somebody if I just don't think they're into what I want them to do.

When I was younger, I used to try and talk people into things. I had this idea that you could sell someone into doing something. But you can't. You can't keep them motivated. You can get them inspired initially. It might work if you're a king like Henry V, and you're trying to get them to just charge into battle, and then they'll figure it out.

But if you're trying to keep someone motivated for the long-term, that motivation has to come intrinsically. You can't just create it, nor can you be the crutch for them if they don't have that intrinsic motivation. So, you have to make sure people actually are high-energy, and want to do what you want them to do, and what you want to work with them on.

Integrity is what someone does, despite what they say they do

Reading signals is very, very important. Signals are what people do despite what they say. So, it's important to pay attention to subtle signals. We all know that socially if someone treats a waiter, or waitress in a restaurant really badly, then it's only a matter of time until they treat you badly.

If somebody screws over an enemy, and is vindictive towards them, well it's only a matter of time before they redefine you from friend to enemy, and you feel their wrath. So, angry, outraged, vindictive, short-term thinking people are essentially that way in many interactions in real life.

People are oddly consistent. That's one of the things you learn about them. So, you want to find long-term people. You want to find people who seem irrationally ethical.

For example, I had a friend of mine whose company I invested in, and the company failed, and he could have wiped out all of the investors. But he kept putting more and more personal money in. Through three different pivots he put personal money in until the company finally succeeded. And in the process, he never wiped out the investors.

And I was always grateful to him for that. I said, "Wow, that's amazing that you were so good to your investors. You didn't wipe them out." And he got offended by that. He said, "I didn't do it for you. I didn't do it for my investors. I did it for me. It's my own self-esteem. It's what I care about. That's how I life my life." That's the kind of person you want to work with.

Another quote that I like, I have a tweet on this. I think I read this somewhere else, so I'm not taking credit for this. But I kind of modified it a little bit. Which is that "self-esteem is the reputation that you have with yourself." You'll always know.

So, good people, moral people, ethical people, easy to work with people, reliable people, tend to have very high self-esteem because they have very good reputations with themselves, and they understand that.

It's not ego. Self-esteem and ego are different things. Because ego can be undeserved, but self-esteem at least you feel like you lived up to your own internal moral code of ethics.

And so it's very hard to work with people who end up being low integrity. And it's hard to figure out who is high integrity and low integrity. Generally, the more someone is saying that they're moral, ethical, and high integrity, the less likely they are to be that way.

It's very much like status signalling. If you overtly bid for status, if you overtly talk about being high status, that is a low status move. If you openly talk about how honest, reliable, and trustworthy you are, you're probably not that honest and trustworthy. That is a characteristic of con men.

So, yeah, pick an industry in which you can play long-term games with long-term people.

10

"Don't partner with cynics and pessimists. Their beliefs are self-fulfilling."

Don't partner with pessimists

Nivi: Let's do this last tweet. You said, "Don't partner with cynics, and pessimists. Their beliefs are self-fulfilling."

Naval: Yes. Essentially, to create things, you have to be a rational optimist. Rational in the sense that you have to see the world for what it really is. And yet you have to be optimistic about your own capabilities, and your capability to get things done.

We all know people who are consistently pessimistic, who will shoot down everything. Everyone in their life has the helpful critical guy, right? He thinks he's being helpful, but he's actually being critical, and he's a downer on everything.

That person will not only never do anything great in their lives, they'll prevent other people around them from doing something great. They think their job is to shoot holes in things. And it's okay to shoot holes in things as long as you come up with a solution.

There's also the classic military line, "Either lead, follow, or get out of the way." And these people want a fourth option, where they don't want to lead, they don't want to follow, but they don't want to get out of the way. They want to tell you why the thing is not going to work.

And all the really successful people I know have a very strong action bias. They just do things. The easiest way to figure out if something is viable or not is by doing it. At least do the first step, and the second step, and the third, and then decide.

So, if you want to be successful in life, creating wealth, or having good relationships, or being fit, or even being happy, you need to have an action bias towards getting what you want.

Partner with rational optimists

And you have to be optimistic about it. Not irrationally. You know, there's nothing worse than someone who is foolhardy and chasing something that's not worth it.

That's why I say rational optimist. But you have to be rational. Know all the pitfalls. Know the downsides, but still keep your chin up.

You've got one life on this planet. Why not try to build something big? This is the beauty of Elon Musk, and why I think he inspires so many people, it's just because he takes on really, really big audacious tasks. And he provides an example for people to think big.

And it takes a lot of work to build even small things. I don't think the corner grocery store owner is working any less hard than Elon Musk, or pouring any less sweat and toil into it. Maybe even more.

But for whatever reason, education, circumstance, they didn't get the chance to think as big, so the outcome is not as big. So, it's just better to think big. Obviously, rationally, within your means, stay optimistic.

The cynics and the pessimists, what they're really saying, it's unfortunate, but they're basically saying, "I've given up. I don't think I can do anything. And so the world to me just looks like a world where nobody can do anything. And so why should you go do something because if you fail, then I'm right, which is great. But if you succeed, then you just make me look bad."

We're descended from pessimists

Nivi: Yes, it's probably better to be an irrational optimist, then it is to be a rational cynic.

Naval: There's a completely rational frame on why you should be an optimist. Historically, if you go back 2,000 years, 5,000 years, 10,000 years, two people are wandering through a jungle, they hear a tiger. One's an optimist, and says, "Oh, it's not headed our way." The other one says, "I'm a pessimist, I'm out of here." And the pessimist runs and survives, and the optimist gets eaten.

So, we're descended from pessimists. We're genetically hardwired to be pessimists. But modern society is far, far safer. There are no tigers wandering around the street. It's very unlikely that you will end up in total ruin, although you should avoid total ruin.

Much more likely that the upside is unlimited, and the downside is limited. So, adapting for modern society means overriding your pessimism, and taking slightly irrationally optimistic bets because the upside is unlimited if you start the next SpaceX, or Tesla, or Uber, you can make billions of dollars of value for society, and for yourself, and change the world.

And if you fail, what's the big deal? You lost a few million dollars of investor money, and they've got plenty more, and that's the bet they take on the chances that you will succeed.

It made sense to be pessimistic in the past. It makes sense to be optimistic today, especially if you're educated and living in a First World country. Even a Third World country. I actually think the economic opportunities in Third World countries are much larger.

The one thing you have to avoid is the risk of ruin. Ruin means stay out of jail. So, don't do anything that's illegal. It's never worth it to wear an orange jumpsuit. And stay out of total catastrophic loss. That could mean that you stay out of things that could be physically dangerous, hurt your body.

You have to watch your health. And stay out of things that can cause you to lose all of your capital, all of your savings. So, don't gamble everything on one go. But take rationally optimistic bets with big upside.

BOCTAOE

Nivi: I think there's people that will try and build up your ideas, and build on your ideas, no matter how far fetched they might seem. And then there are people who list all of the obvious exceptions, no matter how obvious they are.

And fortunately in the startup world, I don't even really get exposed to the people that are giving you the obvious exceptions, and all the reasons it's not going to work. I barely get exposed to that anymore.

Naval: That's what Twitter is for. Scott Adams got so annoyed by this that he came up with a phrase, an acronym, which is "but of course there are obvious exceptions", BOCTAOE. And he used to pin that acronym at the end of his articles for a while.

But Twitter is overrun with nitpickers. Whereas exactly as you were pointing out, Silicon Valley has learned that the upside is so great that you never look down on the kid who's wearing a hoodie and has coffee on his shoes. And just looks like a slob because you don't know if he's going to be the next Mark Zuckerberg, or the next Reid Hoffman.

So, you've got to treat everybody with respect. You've got to look up to every possibility, and opportunity because the upside is so unlimited, and the downside is so limited in the modern world, especially with financial assets and instruments.

11

"Learn to sell. Learn to build. If you can do both, you will be unstoppable."

Learn to sell, learn to build

Nivi: Talking about combining skills, you said that you should "learn to sell, learn to build, if you can do both, you will be unstoppable."

Naval: This is a very broad category. It's two broad categories. One is building the product. Which is hard, and it's multivariate. It can include design, it can include development, it can include manufacturing, logistics, procurement, it can even be designing and operating a service. It has many, many definitions.

But in every industry, there is a definition of the builder. In our tech industry it's the CTO, it's the programmer, it's the software engineer, hardware engineer. But even in the laundry business, it could be the person who's building the laundry service, who is making the trains run on time, who's making sure all the clothes end up in the right place at the right time, and so on.

The other side of it is sales. Again, selling has a very broad definition. Selling doesn't necessarily just mean selling individual customers, but it can mean marketing, it can mean communicating, it can mean recruiting, it can mean raising money, it can mean inspiring people, it could mean doing PR. It's a broad umbrella category.

The Silicon Valley model is a builder and seller

So, generally, the Silicon Valley startup model tends to work best. It's not the only way, but it is probably the most common way, when you have two founders, one of whom is world class at selling, and one of whom is world class at building.

Examples are, of course, Steve Jobs and Steve Wozniak with Apple, Gates and Allen probably had similar responsibilities early on with Microsoft, Larry and Sergey probably broke down along those lines, although it's a little different there because that was a very technical product delivered to end users through a simple interface.

But generally, you will see this pattern repeated over and over. There's a builder and there's a seller. There's a CEO and CTO combo. And venture and technology investors are almost trained to look for this combo whenever possible. It's the magic combination.

If you can do both you will be unstoppable

The ultimate is when one individual can do both. That's when you get true superpowers. That's when you get people who can create entire industries.

The living example is Elon Musk. He may not necessarily be building the rockets himself, but he understands enough that he actually makes technical contributions. He understands the technology well enough that no one's going to snow him on it, and he's not running around making claims that he doesn't think he can't eventually deliver. He may be optimistic on the timelines but he thinks this is within reasonableness for delivery.

Even Steve Jobs developed enough product skills and was involved enough in the product that he also operated in both of these domains. Larry Ellison started as a programmer and I think wrote the first version of Oracle, or was actually heavily involved in it.

Marc Andreessen was also in this domain. He may not have had enough confidence in his sales skills, but he was the programmer who wrote Netscape Navigator, or a big chunk of it. So, I think the real giants in any field are the people who can both build and sell.

I'd rather teach an engineer marketing than a marketer engineering

And usually the building is a thing that a sales person can't pick up later in life. It requires too much focused time. But a builder can pick up selling a little bit later, especially if they were already innately wired to be a good communicator. Bill Gates famously paraphrases this as, "I'd rather teach an engineer marketing, than a marketer engineering."

I think if you start out with a building mentality and you have building skills and it's still early enough in your life, or you have enough focused time that you think you can learn selling, and you have some natural characteristics or you're a good salesperson, then you can double down on those.

Now, your sales skills could be in a different than traditional domain. For example, let's say you're a really good engineer and then people are saying, well, now you need to be good at sales, well, you may not be good at hand-to-hand sales, but you may be a really good writer.

And writing is a skill that can be learned much more easily than, say, in-person selling, and so you may just cultivate writing skills until you become a good online communicator and then use that for your sales.

On the other hand, it could just be that you're a good builder and you're bad at writing and you don't like communicating to mass audiences but you're good one-on-one, so then you might use your sales skills for recruiting or for fundraising, which are more one-on-one kinds of endeavors.

This is pointing out that if you're at the intersection of these two, don't despair because you're not going to be the best technologist and you're not going to be the best salesperson, but in a weird way, that combination, back to the Scott Adams skill stack, that combination of two skills is unstoppable.

Long term, people who understand the underlying product and how to build it and can sell it, these are catnip to investors, these people can break down walls if they have enough energy, and they can get almost anything done.

Nivi: If you could only pick one to be good at, which one would you pick?

Naval: When you're trying to stand out from the noise building is actually better because there're so many hustlers and sales people who have nothing to back them up. When you're starting out, when you're trying to be recognized, building is better.

But much later down the line building gets exhausting because it is a focus job and it's hard to stay current because there's always new people, new products coming up who have newer tools, and frankly more time because it's very intense, it's a very focused task.

So, sales skills actually scale better over time. Like for example, if you have a reputation for building a great product, that's good, but when you ship your new product, I'm going to validate it based on the product. But if you have a reputation for being a good person to do business with and you're persuasive and communicative then that reputation almost becomes self-fulfilling.

So, I think if you only had to pick up one, you can start with building and then transition to selling. This is a cop-out answer, but I think that is actually the right answer.

12

"Arm yourself with specific knowledge,
accountability, and leverage."

Arm yourself with specific knowledge

Nivi: Do you want to talk a little bit about the skills
that you need, in particular specific knowledge,
accountability, leverage and judgment. So, the first
tweet in this area is "Arm yourself with specific
knowledge accountability and leverage." And I'll
throw in judgment as well. I don't think you covered
that in that particular tweet.

Naval: If you want to make money you have to get
paid at scale. And why you, that's accountability, at
scale, that's leverage, and just you getting paid as
opposed to somebody else getting paid , that's
specific knowledge.

So, specific knowledge is probably the hardest thing to get across in this whole tweetstorm, and it's probably the thing that people get the most confused about.

The thing is that we have this idea that everything can be taught, everything can be taught in school. And it's not true that everything can be taught. In fact, the most interesting things cannot be taught.But everything can be learned. And very often that learning either comes from some innate characteristics in your DNA, or it could be through your childhood where you learn soft skills which are very, very hard to teach later on in life, or it's something that is brand new so nobody else knows how to do it either, or it's true on the job training because you're pattern matching into highly complex environments, basically building judgment in a specific domain.

Classic example is investing, but it could be in anything. It could be in judgment in running a fleet of trucks, it could be judgment in weather forecasting.

So, specific knowledge is the knowledge that you care about. Especially if you're later in life, let's say your post 20, 21, 22, you almost don't get to choose which specific knowledge you have. Rather, you get to look at what you have already built by that point in time, and then you can build on top of it.

Specific knowledge can't be trained

The first thing to notice about specific knowledge is that you can't be trained for it. If you can be trained for it, if you can go to a class and learn specific knowledge, then somebody else can be trained for it too, and then we can mass-produce and mass-train people. Heck, we can even program computers to do it and eventually we can program robots to walk around doing it.

So, if that's the case, then you're extremely replaceable and all we have to pay you is the minimum wage that we have to pay you to get you to do it when there are lots of other takers who can be trained to do it. So really, your returns just devolve into your cost of training plus the return on investment on that training.

So, you really want to pick up specific knowledge, you need your schooling, you need your training to be able to capitalize on the best specific knowledge, but the part of it that you're going to get paid for is the specific knowledge.

Specific knowledge is found by pursuing your curiosity

For example, someone who goes and gets a degree in psychology and then becomes a salesperson. Well if they were already a formidable salesperson, a high grade salesmanship to begin with, then the psychology degree is leverage, it arms them and they do much better at sales.

But if they were always an introvert never very good at sales and they're trying to use psychology to learn sales, they're just not going to get that great at it.

So, specific knowledge is found much more by pursuing your innate talents, your genuine curiosity, and your passion. It's not by going to school for whatever it is the hottest job, it's not for going into whatever field investors say is the hottest.

Very often specific knowledge is at the edge of knowledge. It's also stuff that's just being figured out or is really hard to figure out.

So, if you're not 100% into it somebody else who is 100% into it will outperform you. And they won't just outperform you by a little bit, they'll outperform you by a lot because now we're operating the domain of ideas, compound interest really applies and leverage really applies.

So, if you're operating with 1,000 times leverage and somebody is right 80% of the time, and somebody else is right 90% of time, the person who's right 90% of the time will literally get paid hundreds of times more by the market because of the leverage and because of the compounding factors and being correct. So, you really want to make sure you're good at it so that genuine curiosity is very important.

Building specific knowledge will feel like play to you

So, very often, it's not something you sit down and then you reason about, it's more found by observation. You almost have to look back on your own life and see what you're actually good at.

For example, I wanted to be a scientist and that is where a lot of my moral hierarchy comes from. I view scientists sort of at the top of the production chain for humanity. And the group of scientists who have made real breakthroughs and contributions that probably added more to human society, I think, than any single other class of human beings.

Not to take away anything from art or politics or engineering or business, but without the science we'd still be scrambling in the dirt fighting with sticks and trying to start fires.

My whole value system was built around scientists and I wanted to be a great scientist. But when I actually look back at what I was uniquely good at and what I ended up spending my time doing, it was more around making money, tinkering with technology, and selling people on things. Explaining things, talking to people.

So, I have some sales skills, which is a form specific knowledge that I have. I have some analytical skills around how to make money. And I have this ability to absorb data, obsess about it, and break it down and that is a specific skill that I have. I also just love tinkering with technology. And all of this stuff feels like play to me, but it looks like work to others.

So, there are other people to whom these things would be hard and they say like, "Well, how do I get good at being pithy and selling ideas?" Well, if you're not already good at it or if you're not really into it, maybe it's not your thing, focus on the thing that you are really into.

This is ironic, but the first person to actually point out my real specific knowledge was my mother. She did it as an aside, talking from the kitchen and she said it when I was like 15 or 16 years old. I was telling a friend of mine that I want to be an astrophysicist and she said, "No, you're going to go into business."

I was like, "What, my mom's telling me I'm going to be in business. I'm going to be an astrophysicist. Mom doesn't know she's talking about." But mom knew exactly what she was talking about.

She'd already observed that every time we walk down the street, I would critique the local pizza parlor on why they were selling their slices a certain way with certain toppings and why their process of ordering was this way when it should have been that way.

So, she knew that I had more of a business curious mind, but then my obsession with science combined to create technology and technology businesses where I found myself.

So, very often, your specific knowledge is observed and often observed by other people who know you well and revealed in situations rather than something that you come up with.

13

Specific knowledge is knowledge that you cannot be trained for. If society can train you, it can train someone else, and replace you.

Discussed in chapter 12.

14

. . . .

"Specific knowledge is found by pursuing your genuine curiosity and passion rather than whatever is hot right now."

. . . .

Discussed in <u>chapter 12</u>.

15

"Building specific knowledge will feel like play to you but will look like work to others."

Discussed in <u>chapter 12</u>.

16

"When specific knowledge is taught, it's through apprenticeships, not schools."

Discussed in <u>chapter 17</u>.

17

"Specific knowledge is often highly technical or creative. It cannot be outsourced or automated."

Specific knowledge can be taught through apprenticeships

Naval: To the extent that specific knowledge is taught, it's on the job. It's through apprenticeships. And that's why the best businesses, the best careers are the apprenticeship Or self-taught careers, because those are things society still has not figured out how to train and automate yet.

The classic line here is that Warren Buffett went to Benjamin Graham when he got out of school. Benjamin Graham was the author of the Intelligent Investor and sort of modernized or created value investing as a discipline. And Warren Buffett went to

Benjamin Graham and offered to work for him for free.

And Graham said, "Actually, you're overpriced, free is overpriced." And Graham was absolutely right. When it comes to a very valuable apprenticeship like the type that Graham was going to give Buffet, Buffet should have been paying him a lot of money. That right there tells you that those are skills worth having.

Specific knowledge is often highly creative or technical

Specific knowledge also tends to be technical and creative. It's on the bleeding edge of technology, on the bleeding edge of art, on the bleeding edge of communication.

Even today, for example, there are probably meme lords out there on the Internet who can create incredible memes that will spread the idea to millions of people. Or are very persuasive – Scott Adams is a good example of this. He is essentially becoming one of the most credible people in the world by making accurate predictions through persuasive arguments and videos.

And that is specific knowledge that he has built up over the years because he got obsessed with hypnosis when he was young, he learned how to communicate through cartooning, he embraced Periscope early, so he's been practicing lots of conversation, he's read all the books on the topic, he's employed in his everyday life. If you look at his girlfriend, she's this beautiful young Instagram model.

That is an example of someone who has built up a specific knowledge over the course of his career. It's highly creative, it has elements of being technical in it, and it's something that is never going to be automated.

No one's going to take that away from him, because he's also accountable under one brand as Scott Adams, and he's operating with the leverage of media with Periscope and drawing Dilbert cartoons and writing books. He has massive leverage on top of that brand and he can build wealth out of it if he wanted to build additional wealth beyond what he already has.

Specific knowledge is specific to the individual and situation

Nivi: Should we be calling it unique knowledge or does specific knowledge somehow make more sense for it?

Naval: You know, I came up with this framework when I was really young. We're talking decades and decades. It's now probably over 30 years old. So the time specific knowledge stuck with me so that . how I think about it.

The reason I didn't try and change it is because every other term that I found for it was overloaded in a different way. At least specific knowledge isn't that used. I can kind of rebrand it.

The problem with unique knowledge is, yeah, maybe it's unique but if I learn it from somebody else it's longer unique, then we both know it. So, it's not so much that it is unique, it's that it is highly specific to the situation, it's specific to the individual, it's specific to the problem, and it can only be built as part of a larger obsession, interest, and time spent in that domain.

It can't just be read straight out of a single book, nor can it be taught in a single course, nor can it be programmed into a single algorithm.

You can't be too deliberate about assembling specific knowledge

Nivi: Speaking of Scott Adams, he's got a blog post on how to build your career by getting in, say, the top 25 percentile at three or more things. And by doing that, you become the only person in the world who can do those three things in the 25th percentile.

So, instead of trying to be the best at one thing, you just try to be very, very good at three or more things. Is that a way of building specific knowledge?

Naval: I actually think the best way is just to follow your own obsession. And somewhere in the back of your mind, you can realize that, actually, this obsession I like and I'll keep an eye out for the commercial aspects of it.

But I think if you go around trying to build it a little too deliberately, if you become too goal-oriented on the money, then you won't pick the right thing. You won't actually pick the thing that you love to do, so you won't go deep enough into it.

Scott Adams' observation is a good one, predicated on statistics. Let's say there's 10,000 areas that are valuable to the human race today in terms of knowledge to have, and the number one in those 10,000 slots is taken.

Someone else is likely to be the number one in each of those 10,000, unless you happen to be one of the 10,000 most obsessed people in the world that at a given thing.

But when you start combining, well, number 3,728 with top-notch sales skills and really good writing skills and someone who understands accounting and finance really well, when the need for that intersection arrives, you've expanded enough from

10,000 through combinatorics to millions or tens of millions. So, it just becomes much less competitive.

Also, there's diminishing returns. So, it's much easier to be top 5 percentile at three or four things than it is to be literally the number one at something.

Build specific knowledge where you are a natural

I think it's a very pragmatic approach. But I think it's important that one not start assembling things too deliberately because you do want to pick things where you are a natural. Everyone is a natural at something.

We're all familiar with that phrase, a natural. "Oh, this person is a natural at meeting men or women, this person is a natural socialite, this person is a natural programmer, this person is a natural reader." So, whatever you are a natural at, you want to double down on that.

And then there are probably multiple things you're natural at because personalities and humans are very complex. So, we want to be able to take the things that you are natural at and combine them so that you automatically, just through sheer interest and enjoyment, end up top 25% or top 10% or top 5% at a number of things.

18

. . . .

"Embrace accountability, and take business risks
under your own name. Society will reward you with
responsibility, equity, and leverage."

. . . .

You have to have accountability to get leverage

Nivi: Why don't we jump into accountability, which
I thought was pretty interesting and I think you have
your own unique take on it. So the first tweet on
accountability was, "Embrace accountability and
take business risks under your own name. Society
will reward you with responsibility, equity, and
leverage."

Naval: Yeah. So to get rich, you're going to need
leverage. Leverage comes in labor, comes in capital,
or it can come through code or media. But most of
these, like labor and capital, people have to give to
you. For labor, somebody has to follow you. For

capital, somebody has to give you money or assets to manage or machines.

So to get these things, you have to build up credibility and you have to do those under your own name as much as possible, which is risky. So accountability is a double-edged thing. It allows you to take credit when things go well and to bear the brunt of the failure when things go badly.

Take business risks under your own name

So in that sense, people who are stamping their names on things aren't foolish. They're just confident. Maybe it turns out to be foolish in the end, but if you look at a Kanye or an Oprah or a Trump or an Elon or anyone like that, these people can get rich just off their name because their name is such powerful branding.

Regardless of what you think of Trump, you have to realize that the guy was among the best in the world at just branding his name. Why would you go to Trump Casino? Used to be because Trump. Why would you go to a Trump tower? Because of Trump.

When it came time to vote, I think that a lot of voters just went in and said, "Trump." They recognize the name, so the name recognition paid off.

Same thing with Oprah. She puts her brand on something, her name on something and it flies off the shelves, and it's like an instant validator.

These people also take risks for putting their name out there. Obviously Trump is now probably hated by half or more than half of the country and by a big chunk of the world as he sticks his name out there.

By putting your name out there, you become a celebrity, and fame has many, many downsides. It's better to be anonymous and rich than to be poor and famous, but even famous and rich has a lot of downsides associated with it. You're always in the public eye.

A well-functioning team has clear accountability for each position

Accountability is quite important, and when you're working to build a product or you're working in a team or you're working in a business, we constantly have drummed into our heads how important it is to be part of a team. Absolutely agree with that.

A lot of our training socially is telling us to not stick our necks out of the crowd. There's a saying that I hear from our Australian friends that the tall poppy gets cut. Don't stick your neck out, but I would say that actually a really, really well-functioning team is small and has clear accountability for each of the different portions.

You can say, "Okay, this person's responsible for building the product. This person's responsible for the messaging. This person's responsible for raising money. This person's responsible for the pricing strategy and maybe the online advertising." So if somebody screws up, you know exactly who's responsible. While at the same time if something goes really well, you also know exactly who's responsible.

If you have a small team and you have clearly delineated responsibilities, then you can still keep a very high level of accountability. Accountability is really important because when something succeeds or fails, if it fails, everybody points fingers at each other, and if it succeeds, everybody steps forward to take credit.

We've all had that experience when we were in school and we got a group assignment to do. There were probably a few people in there who did a lot of the work. Then there are a few people who just did a lot of grandstanding or positioning to do the work. We're all familiar with this from a childhood sense, but it's sort of uncomfortable to talk about.

People who can fail in public have a lot of power

Clear accountability is important. Without accountability, you don't have incentives. Without accountability, you can't build credibility. But you take risk. You take risk of failure. You take risk of humiliation. You take risk of failure under your own name.

Luckily in modern society, there's no more debtors' prison and people don't go to jail or get executed for losing other people's money, but we're still socially hard wired to not fail in public under our own names. The people who have the ability to fail in public under their own names actually gain a lot of power .

For example, I'll give a personal anecdote. Up until about 2013, 2014, my public persona was an entirely around startups and investing. Only around 2014, 2015 did I start talking about philosophy and psychological things and broader things.

It made me a little nervous because I was doing it under my own name. There were definitely people in the industry who sent me messages through the back channel like, "What are you doing? You're ending your career. This is stupid."

I kind of just went with it. I took a risk. Same with crypto. Early on, I took a risk.

But when you put your name out there, you take a risk with certain things. You also get to reap the rewards. You get the benefits.

19

The most accountable people have singular, public, and risky brands: Oprah, Trump, Kanye, Elon.

Discussed in chapter 18.

20

"Give me a lever long enough, and a place to stand, and I will move the earth."
- Archimedes

Our brains aren't evolved to comprehend new forms of leverage

Nivi: Why don't we talk a little bit about leverage?

The first tweet in the storm was a famous quote from Archimedes, which was, "Give me a lever long enough and a place to stand and I will move the Earth."

The next tweet was, "Fortunes require leverage. Business leverage comes from capital, people and products with no marginal costs of replication."

Naval: Leverage is critical. The reason I stuck in Archimedes quote in there is… normally I don't like putting other people's quotes in my Twitter. That doesn't add any value. You can go look up those people's quotes. But this quote I had to put in there because it's just so fundamental. I read it when I was very, very young and it had a huge impression on me.

We all know what leverage is when we use a seesaw or a lever. We understand how that works physically, but I think what our brains aren't really well-evolved to comprehend is how much leverage is possible in modern society and what the newest forms of leverage are.

Society overvalues labor leverage

The oldest form of leverage is labor, which is people working for you. Instead of me lifting rocks, I can have 10 people lift rocks. Then just by my guidance on where the rock should go, a lot more rocks get moved than I could do myself. Everybody understands this because we're evolved to understand the labor form of leverage, so what happens is society overvalues labor as a form of leverage.

This is why your parents are impressed when you get a promotion and you have lots of people working underneath you. This is why when a lot of naive people, when you tell them about your company, they'll say, "How many people work there?" They'll use that as a way to establish credibility. They're trying to measure how much leverage and impact you actually have.

Or when someone starts a movement, they'll say how many people they have or how big the army is. We just automatically assume that more people is better.

You want the minimum amount of labor that allows you to use the other forms of leverage

I would argue that this is the worst form of leverage that you could possibly use. Managing other people is incredibly messy. It requires tremendous leadership skills. You're one short hop from a mutiny or getting eaten or torn apart by the mob.

It's incredibly competed over. Entire civilizations have been destroyed over this fight. For example, communism, Marxism, is all about the battle between capital and labor, das kapital and das labor. It's kind of a trap.

You really want to stay out of labor-based leverage. You want the minimum amount of people working with you that are going to allow to use the other forms of leverage, which I would argue are much more interesting.

Capital has been the dominant form of leverage in

The second type of leverage is capital. This one's a little less hardwired into us because large amounts of money moving around and being saved and being invested in money markets, these are inventions of human beings the in last few hundred to few thousand years. They're not evolved with us from hundreds of thousands of years.

We understand them a little bit less well. They probably require more intelligence to use correctly, and the ways in which we use them keep changing. Management skills from a hundred years ago might still apply today, but investing in the stock market skills from a hundred years ago probably don't apply to the same level today.

Capital is a trickier form of leverage to use. It's more modern. It's the one that people have used to get fabulously wealthy in the last century. It's probably been the dominant form of leverage in the last century.

You can see this by who are the richest people. It's bankers, politicians in corrupt countries who print money, essentially people who move large amounts of money around.

If you look at the top of very large companies, outside of technology companies, in many, many large old companies, the CEO job is really a financial job. They're really financial asset managers. Sometimes, an asset manager can put a pleasant face on it, so you get a Warren Buffet type.

But deep down, I think we all dislike capital as a form of leverage because it feels unfair. It's this invisible thing that can be accumulated and passed across generations and suddenly seems to result in people having gargantuan amounts of money with nobody else around them or necessarily sharing in it.

That said, capital is a powerful form of leverage. It can be converted to labor. It can be converted to other things. It's very surgical, very analytical.

If you are a brilliant investor and give $1 billion and you can make a 30% return with it, whereas anybody else can only make a 20% return, you're going to get all the money and you're going to get paid very handsomely for it.

It scales very, very well. If you get good at managing capital, you can manage more and more capital much more easily than you can manage more and more people.

You need specific knowledge and accountability to obtain capital

It is a good form of leverage, but the hard part with capital is how do you obtain it? That's why I talked about specific knowledge and accountability first.

If you have specific knowledge in a domain and if you're accountable and you have a good name in that domain, then people are going to give you capital as a form of leverage that you can use to then go get more capital.

Capital also is fairly well understood. I think a lot of the knocks against capitalism come because of the accumulation of capital.

21

"Fortunes require leverage. Business leverage comes from capital, people, and products with no marginal cost of replication (code and media)."

Discussed in <u>chapter 20</u>.

22

. . . .

"Capital means money. To raise money, apply your specific knowledge, with accountability, and show resulting good judgment."

. . . .

Discussed in <u>chapter 20</u>.

23

"Labor means people working for you. It's the oldest and most fought-over form of leverage. Labor leverage will impress your parents, but don't waste your life chasing it."

Discussed in chapter 20.

24

"Capital and labor are permissioned leverage. Everyone is chasing capital, but someone has to give it to you. Everyone is trying to lead, but someone has to follow you."

Discussed in chapter 20.

25

"Code and media are permissionless leverage. They're the leverage behind the newly rich. You can create software and media that works for you while you sleep."

Product and media are the new leverage

Naval: The most interesting and the most important form of leverage is this idea of products that have no marginal cost of replication. This is the new form of leverage.

This was only invented in the last few hundred years. It got started with the printing press. It accelerated with broadcast media, and now it's really blown up with the Internet and with coding.

Now, you can multiply your efforts without having to involve other humans and without needing money from other humans.

This podcast is a form of leverage. Long ago, I would have had to sit in a lecture hall and lecture each of you personally. I would have maybe reached a few hundred people and that would have been that.

Then 40 years ago, 30 years ago, I would have to be lucky to get on TV, which is somebody else's leverage. They would have distorted the message. They would taken the economics out of it or charged me for it. They would have muddled the message, and I would have been lucky to get that form of leverage.

Today, thanks to the Internet, I can buy a cheap microphone, hook it up to a laptop or an iPad, and there you are all listening.

Product leverage is where the new fortunes are made

This newest form of leverage is where all the new fortunes are made, all the new billionaires. The last generation, fortunes were made by capital. That was the Warren Buffets of the world.

But the new generation's fortunes are all made through code or media. Joe Rogan making 50 to a 100 million bucks a year from his podcast. You're going to have a PewDiePie. I don't know how much money he's rolling in, but he's bigger than the news. The Fortnite players. Of course Jeff Bezos and Mark Zuckerberg and Larry Page and Sergey Brin and Bill

Gates and Steve Jobs. That is all code-based leverage.

Combining all three forms of leverage is a magic combination

Now, the beauty is when you combine all of these three. That's where tech startups really excel, where you take just the minimum, but highest output labor that you can get, which are engineers, and designers, product developers. Then you add in capital. You use that for marketing, advertising, scaling. You add in lots of code and media and podcasts and content to get it all out there.

That is a magic combination, and that's why you see technology startups explode out of nowhere, use massive leverage and just make huge outsize returns.

Product and media leverage are permissionless

Nivi: Do you want to talk a little bit about permissioned versus permissionless?

Naval: Probably the most interesting thing to keep in mind about the new forms of leverage is they are permissionless. They don't require somebody else's permission for you to use them or succeed.

For labor leverage, somebody has to decide to follow you. For capital leverage, somebody has to give you money to invest or to turn into a product.

Coding, writing books, recording podcasts, tweeting, YouTubing, these kinds of things, these are permissionless. You don't need anyone's permission to do them, and that's why they are very egalitarian. They're great equalizers of leverage.

As much as people may rail on Facebook and YouTube, they're not going to stop using it because this permissionless leverage, where everyone can be a broadcaster, is just too good.

The same way you can rail upon Apple for having a slightly closed ecosystem in the iPhone, but everyone's writing apps for it. As long as you can write apps for it, you can get rich or reach users doing that, why not?

The robot army is already here—code lets you tell them what to do

I think of all the forms of leverage, the best one in modern society … This is glib. This is a little overused. This is why I tell people learn to code. It's that we have this idea that in the future there's going to be these robots and they're going to be doing everything.

That may be true, but I would say that the majority of the robot revolution has already happened. The robots are already here and there are way more robots than there are humans, it's just that we pack them in data centers for heat and efficiency reasons. We put them in servers. They're inside the computers. All the circuits, it's robot minds inside that's doing all the work.

Every great software developer, for example, now has an army of robots working for him at nighttime, while he or she sleeps, after they've written the code and it's just cranking away.

The robot army is already here. The robot revolution has already happened. We're about halfway through it. We're just adding in much more of the hardware component these days as we get more comfortable with the idea of autonomous vehicles and autonomous airplanes and autonomous ships and maybe autonomous trucks. There're delivery bots and Boston Dynamics robots and all that.

But robots who are doing web searching for you, for example, are already here. The ones who are cleaning up your video and audio and transmitting it around the world are already here. The ones who are answering many customer service queries, things that you would have had to call a human for are already here.

An army of robots is already here. It's very cheaply available. The bottleneck is just figuring out intelligent and interesting things to do to them.

Essentially you can order this army of robots around. The commands have to be issued in a computer language, in a language that they understand.

These robots aren't very smart. They have to be told very precisely what to do and how to do it. Coding is such a great superpower because now you can speak the language of the robot armies and you can tell them what to do.

Nivi: I think at this point, people are not only commanding the army of robots within servers through code, they're actually manipulating the movement of trucks, of other people. Just ordering a package on Amazon, you're manipulating the movement of many people and many robots to get a package delivered to you.

People are doing the same things to build businesses now. There's the army of robots within servers and then there's also an army of actual robots and people that are being manipulated through software.

26

"An army of robots is freely available - it's just packed in data centers for heat and space efficiency. Use it."

Discussed in chapter 25.

27

....

"If you can't code, write books and blogs, record videos and podcasts."

....

Discussed in chapter 25.

28

. . . .

"Leverage is a force multiplier for your judgement."

. . . .

In an age of infinite leverage, judgment becomes the most important skill

Nivi: We spoke about specific knowledge, we talked about accountability, we talked about leverage. The last skill that Naval talks about in his tweetstorm is judgment, where he says, that "Leverage is a force multiplier for your judgment."

Naval: We are now living in an age of nearly infinite leverage, and all the great fortunes are created through leverage. Your first job is to go and obtain leverage, and you can obtain leverage through permission by getting people to work for you, or by raising capital.

Or you can get leverage permissionlessly by learning how to code or becoming good communicator and podcasting, broadcasting, creating videos, writing, etc.

That's how you get leverage, but once you have leverage, what do you do with it? Well, the first part of your career's spent hustling to get leverage. Once you have the leverage, then you wanna slow down a bit, because your judgment really matters.

It's like you've gone from steering your sailboat around to now you're steering an ocean liner or a tanker. You have a lot more at risk, but you have a lot more to gain as well. You're carrying a much higher payload. In an age of infinite leverage, judgment becomes the most important skill.

Warren Buffett is so wealthy now because of his judgment. Even if you were to take away all of Warren's money, tomorrow, investors would come out of the woodwork and hand him a $100 billion because they know his judgment is so good, and they would give him a big chunk of that $100 billion to invest.

Everything else you do is setting you up to apply judgment

Ultimately, everything else that you do is actually setting you up to apply your judgment. One of the big things that people rail on is CEO pay. For sure there's crony capitalism that goes on where these

CEOs control their boards and the boards give them too much money.

But, there are certain CEOs who definitely earned their keep because their judgment is better. If you're steering a big ship, if you're steering Google or Apple, and your judgment is 10 or 20 percent better than the next person's, society will literally pay you hundreds of millions of dollars more, because you're steering a $100 billion ship.

If you're on course 10 or 20 percent of the time more often than the other person, the compounding results on that hundreds of billions of dollars you're managing will be so large that your CEO pay will be dwarfed in comparison.

Demonstrated judgment, credibility around the judgment, is so critical. Warren Buffett wins here because he has massive credibility. He's been highly accountable. He's been right over and over in the public domain. He's built a reputation for very high integrity, so you can trust him.

A person like that, people will throw infinite leverage behind him because of his judgment. Nobody asks him how hard he works; nobody asks him when he wakes up or when he goes to sleep. They're like, "Warren, just do your thing."

Judgment, especially demonstrated judgment, with high accountability, clear track record, is critical.

Judgment is knowing the long-term consequences of your actions

Nivi: Let's define judgment. I would define it as knowing the long-term effects of your decisions, or being able to predict the long-term effects of your decisions.

Naval: It's funny. My definition of wisdom is knowing the long term consequences of your actions, so they're not all that different. Wisdom is just judgment on a personal domain.

Wisdom applied to external problems I think is judgment. They're highly linked. But, yes, it's knowing the long term consequences of your actions and then making the right decision to capitalize on that.

Without experience, judgment is often less than useless

Judgment is very hard to build up. This is where both intellect and experience come in play.

There are many problems with the so-called intellectuals in the ivory tower, but one of the reasons why Nassim Taleb rails against them is because they have no skin in the game. They have no real-world experience, so they just apply purely intellect.

Intellect without any experience is often worse than useless because you get the confidence that the intellect gives you, and you get some of the credibility, but because you had no skin in the game, and you had no real experience, and no real accountability, you're just throwing darts.

The real world is always far, far more complex than we can intellectualize. Especially all the interesting, fast-moving edge domains and problems, you can't get there without experience. If you are smart and you iterate fast, it's not even you put 10,000 hours into something, but you take 10,000 tries at something.

The people with the best judgment are among the least emotional

If you are smart and you have a lot of quick iterations, and you try to keep your emotions out of it, the people with the best judgment are actually among the least emotional. A lot of the best investors are considered almost robotic in that regard, but I wouldn't be surprised if even the best entrepreneurs often come across as unemotional.

There is sort of this archetype of the passionate entrepreneur, and yeah, they have to care about what they're doing, but they also have to see very clearly what's actually happening. The thing that prevents you from seeing what's actually happening are your emotions. Our emotions are constantly clouding our judgment, and in investing, or in running companies, or in building products, or being an entrepreneur, emotions really get in the way.

Emotions are what prevent you from seeing what's actually happening, until you can no longer resist the truth of what's happening, until it becomes too sudden, and then you're forced into suffering; which is sort of a breaking of this fantasy that you had put together.

Nivi: To try and connect some of these concepts, I would say that, first, you're accountable for your judgment. Judgment is the exercise of wisdom. Wisdom comes from experience; and that experience can be accelerated through short iterations.

A lot of the top investors often sound like philosophers

Naval: And the reason why a lot of the top investors, a lot of the value investors, like if you read Jeremy Grantham, or you read Warren Buffet, or you read up on Michael Burry, these people sound like philosophers, or they are philosophers, or they're reading a lot of history books or science books.

Like what are they doing, shouldn't they be reading investment books. No. Investment books are the worst place to learn about investment, because investment is a real-world activity that is highly multi-variate, all the advantages are always being competed away. It's always on the cutting-edge.

What you actually just need is very, very broad-based judgment and thinking. The best way to do that is to study everything, including a lot of philosophy. Philosophy also makes you more stoic, makes you less emotional, and so you make better decisions; you have better judgment.

The more outraged someone is, the worse their judgment

One simple thing is I see … I go out on Twitter and it seems like half of Twitter is outraged at something at all times. You can go within someone's Twitter feed and get at least some semblance of what it must be like to be in their head all the time.

The more outraged somebody is, I guarantee you, the worse their judgment is. If someone's constantly tweeting political outrage, and just see like an angry person getting into fights, you don't want to hand this person the keys to your car, let alone the keys to your company.

29

"Judgement requires experience, but can be built faster by learning foundational skills."

Discussed in <u>chapter 28</u>.

30

"There is no skill called "business." Avoid business magazines and business classes."

Read what you love until you love to read

Nivi: Before we go and talk about accountability and leverage and judgment, you've got a few tweets further down the line that I would put in the category of continuous learning.

They're essentially, "there is no skill called business. Avoid business magazines and business class, study microeconomics, game theory, psychology, persuasion, ethics, mathematics and computers."

There's one other comment that you made in a Periscope that was, "you should be able to pick up any book in the library and read it." And the last tweet in this category was, "reading is faster than listening, doing is faster than watching."

Naval: Yeah, the most important tweet on this, I don't even have in here unfortunately, which is, the foundation of learning is reading. I don't know a smart person who doesn't read and read all the time.

And the problem is, what do I read? How do I read? Because for most people it's a struggle, it's a chore. So, the most important thing is just to learn how to educate yourself and the way to educate yourself is to develop a love for reading.

So, the tweet that is left out, the one that I was hinting at is, "read what you love until you love to read." It's that simple.

Everybody I know who reads a lot loves to read, and they love to read because they read books that they loved. It's a little bit of a catch-22, but you basically want to start off just reading wherever you are and then keep building up from there until reading becomes a habit. And then eventually, you will just get bored of the simple stuff.

So you may start off reading fiction, then you might graduate to science fiction, then you may graduate to non-fiction, then you may graduate to science, or philosophy, or mathematics or whatever it is, but take your natural path and just read the things that interest you until you kind of understand them. And then you'll naturally move to the next thing and the next thing and the next thing.

Read the original scientific books in a field

Now, there is an exception to this, which is where I was hinting with what things you actually do want to learn, which is, at some point there's too much out there to read. Even reading is full of junk.

There are actually things you can read, especially early on, that will program your brain a certain way, and then later things that you read, you will decide whether those things are true or false based on the earlier things.

So, it is important that you read foundational things. And foundational things, I would say, are the original books in a given field that are very scientific in their nature.

For example, instead of reading a business book, pick up Adam Smith's The Wealth of Nations. Instead of reading a book on biology or evolution that's written today, I would pick up Darwin's Origin of the Species. Instead of reading a book on biotech right now that may be very advanced, I would just pick up The Eighth Day of Creation by Watson and Crick. Instead of reading advanced books on what cosmology and what Neil Degrasse Tyson and Stephen Hawking have been saying, you can pick up

Richard Feynman's Six Easy Pieces and start with basic physics.

Don't fear any book

If you understand the basics, especially in mathematics and physics and sciences, then you will not be afraid of any book. All of us have that memory of when we were sitting in class and we're learning mathematics, and it was all logical and all made sense until at one point the class moved too fast and we fell behind.

Then after that we were left memorizing equations, memorizing concepts without being able to derive them from first principles. And at that moment, we're lost, because unless you're a professional mathematician, you're not going to remember those things. All you're going to remember are the techniques, the foundations.

So, you have to make sure that you're building on a steel frame of understanding because you're putting together a foundation for skyscraper, and you're not just memorizing things because you're just memorizing things you're lost. So the foundations are ultra important.

And the ultimate, the ultimate is when you walk into a library and you look at it up and down and you don't fear any book. You know that you can take any book off the shelf, you can read it, you can understand it, you can absorb what is true, you can reject what is false, and you have a basis for even working that out that is logical and scientific and not purely just based on opinions.

The means of learning are abundant, the desire to learn is scarce

The beauty of the internet is the entire library of Alexandria times 10 is at your fingertips at all times. It's not the means of education or the means of learning are scarce, the means of learning are abundant. It's the desire to learn that's scarce. So, you really have to cultivate the desire.

And it's not even cultivating you've to not lose it. Children have a natural curiosity. If you go to a young child who's first learning language, they're pretty much always asking: What's this? What's that? Why is this? Who's that? They're always asking questions.

But one of the problems is that schools and our educational system, and even our way of raising children replaces curiosity with compliance. And once you replace the curiosity with the compliance, you get an obedient factory worker, but you no longer get a creative thinker. And you need creativity, you need the ability to feed your own brain to learn whatever you want.

31

"Study microeconomics, game theory, psychology, persuasion, ethics, mathematics, and computers."

Discussed in <u>chapter 30</u>.

32

"Reading is faster than listening. Doing is faster than watching."

Discussed in <u>chapter 30</u>.

33

"You should be too busy to "do coffee," while still keeping an uncluttered calendar."

Be too busy to "do coffee" while keeping an uncluttered calendar

Naval: Then we squander our time with the death of 1,000 cuts. Another tweet I had was, "You should be too busy to do coffee, while still keeping an uncluttered calendar." People who know me, know that I'm famous for simultaneously doing two things. One is having a very clean calendar. I have almost no meetings on it.

There are people that I meet with, when they see my calendar they almost weep, while at the same time, I am busy all the time. I'm always doing something. It's usually "work-related" but it is whatever the highest impact thing is that needs to be done at that time and that I'm most interested or inspired about. But the only way to do that is to constantly, ruthlessly decline meetings.

People want to do coffee and build relationships, and that's fine early in your career when you're still exploring. But later in your career when you're exploiting, and there are more things coming at you than you have time for, you have to ruthlessly cut meetings out of your life.

If someone wants to do a meeting, see if you can do it with a phone call instead. If they want to do a phone call, see if they can do it with an email instead. If they want to do with email, see if they can do with a text message instead. If they're text messaging, you should probably be ignoring most text messages unless they're urgent, true emergencies.

One has to be utterly ruthless about dodging meetings. When you do do meetings, do walking meetings, do standing meetings. Keep them short, keep them actionable, keep them small. Any meeting with eight people sitting around at a conference table, nothing is getting done in that meeting. You are literally just dying one hour at a time.

Nivi: "Doing coffee" reminds me of a old quote, I think from Steve Jobs, when they asked him, "Hey, why doesn't Apple come to conventions?" Or "Why don't you come to my convention?" His response was, "Well, then because we wouldn't be here working."

Naval: Yeah, I used to have a tough time turning people down for meetings, but now I just tell them outright. I just say, "Look, I don't do non-transactional meetings. I don't do meetings without a strict agenda. I don't do meetings unless we absolutely have to."

Nivi used to do this. He would email people when they would ask Nivi and I for a coffee meeting, to get to know you. He would say, "We don't do meetings unless it's life and death urgent." And then that person has to basically respond, "Yeah, it's life and death urgent" or there's no meeting.

People will meet with you when you have proof of work

When you have something important or something valuable, other busy, interesting people will meet with you. Your calling card has to be, "Hey, here's what I've done. Here's what I can show you. Let's meet and I'll be respectful of your time if this is useful to you."

I find that there are very busy important people who will take your meeting, but you have to come with a proper calling card. All the people who tweet and who email famous or rich people saying, "Hey, if I could just get one meeting with you," and they're vague about it, they're not going to get anywhere in life.

You have to build up the credibility. When, for example, an investor in the tech business and the venture business looks at a startup, the first thing they want to see is, they want to see some evidence of product progress. They don't just want to even see a slide deck, they want to see a product progress, because the product progress is the resume for the entrepreneur. It is the unshakable, unfake-able resume.

You have to do the work. To use a crypto analogy, you have to have proof of work. If you have proof of work, and you truly have something interesting, then you shouldn't hesitate to put it together in an email and send it to somebody. Even then, when you're asking for a meeting, you wanna be super actionable about it.

Networking is overrated even early in your career

But I would say, even if you yourself haven't made it yet, if you think you're going to make it by going out and networking and doing a whole bunch of meetings, you're probably incorrect. Yes, networking can be important early in your career, and yes you can get serendipitous with meetings, but the odds are pretty low.

As we spent time talking about earlier, when you are just meeting people and hoping to get that lucky break, you're relying on Type One Luck, which is Blind Luck, and Type Two Luck, which is Hustle Luck.

But what you're not getting, is Type Three or Type Four Luck, which are the better kinds where you spend time developing a reputation, working on something; developing a unique point of view, and being able to spot opportunities that others can't.

A busy calendar and a busy mind will destroy your ability to do great things in this world. If you want to be able to do great things, whether you're a musician, or whether you are an entrepreneur, or whether you're an investor, you need free time and you need a free mind.

34

"Set and enforce an aspirational personal hourly rate. If fixing a problem will save less than your hourly rate, ignore it. If outsourcing a task will cost less than your hourly rate, outsource it."

Set and enforce an aspirational hourly rate

Nivi: We covered the skills that you need to get rich. That was specific knowledge, accountability, leverage, judgment, and life-long learning. Let's talk a little bit about the importance of working hard and valuing your time.

Naval: No one is going to value you more than you value yourself. You just have to set a very high personal hourly rate and you have to stick to it. Even since I was young, I just decided I was worth a lot more than the market though I was worth, but I started treating myself that way.

Always factor your time into every decision. How much time does it take? Oh it's gonna take me an hour to get across town to get this thing. I value myself at a $100 an hour; that's basically throwing $100 out of my pocket. Am I going to do that?

You buy something from Amazon; they screwed it up, you have to return it. Is it worth your time to return it? Is it worth the mental hassle? Keep in mind that you have less work hours, you have less mentally high-output hours. Do you want to use them to run errands and solve little problems, or do you want to save them for the big stuff?

All the great scientists were terrible at managing their household life. None of them had a clean, organized room, or made all their social events on time, or sent their thank you cards.

You can't penny pinch your way to wealth

You can spend your life however you want, but if you want to get rich, it has to be your number one overwhelming desire. Which means, it has to come before anything else; which means you can't be penny-pinching. This is what people don't understand.

You can penny-pinch your way to a basic sustenance. You can keep your expenses low, maybe retire early and not spend too much. That's perfectly valid. But we're here to talk about wealth creation. If you're going to do that, then that has to be your number one overwhelming priority.

My aspirational rate was $5,000/hr

Fast forward to your wealthy self and pick some intermediate hourly rate. For me, believe it or not, back when you could have hired me … Which now obviously you can't, but back when you could have hired me … this was true a decade ago or even two decades ago, before I had any real money. My hourly rate, I used to say to myself over and over is, $5,000 an hour. Today when I look back, really it was about $1,000 an hour [back then].

Of course, I still ended up doing stupid things, like arguing with the electrician, or returning the broken speaker, but I shouldn't have, and I did a lot less than any of my friends would. I would make a theatrical show out of throwing something in the trash pile, or giving it to Salvation Army, rather than trying to return it, or handing something to people rather than trying to fix it.

I would argue with my girlfriends, and even today it's my wife, "I don't do that. That's not a problem that I solve." I still argue that, with my mother, when she hands me little to-do's. I just don't do that. I would rather hire you an assistant. This was true even when I didn't have money.

If you can outsource something for less than your hourly rate, do it

Another way of thinking about something is, if you can outsource something or not do something for less than your hourly rate, outsource it or don't do it. If you can hire someone to do it for less than your hourly rate, hire them. That even includes things like cooking. You may want to eat your healthy home cooked meals, but if you can outsource it, do that instead.

I know some people will say, "Well what about the joy of life? What about getting it right just your way?" Sure, you can do that, but you're not gonna be wealthy because now you've made something else a priority.

Paul Graham basically said it pretty well for Y Combinator startups, he said, "You should be working on your product and getting product-market fit. And you should be exercising and eating healthy." That's about it. That's all you have time for while you're on this mission.

Your hourly rate should seem absurdly high

Set a very high hourly aspirational rate for yourself and stick to it. It should seem and feel absurdly high.

If it doesn't, it's not high enough. Whatever you picked, my advice to you would be to raise it. Like I said, for myself, even before I had money, for the longest time I used $5,000 an hour. And if you extrapolate that out into what it looks like as an annual salary, it's the multiple millions of dollars per year.

Ironically, I actually think I've beaten it. I'm not the hardest working person; I'm actually a lazy person. I work through bursts of energy where I'm really motivated with something. If I actually look at how much I've earned per actual hour that I've put in, it's probably quite a bit higher than that.

35

"Work as hard as you can. Even though who you work with and what you work on are more important than how hard you work."

Work as hard as you can

Naval: Let's talk about hard work. There's this battle that happens in Twitter a lot between, should you work hard and should you not. David Hauser's (correction: David Heinemeier Hansson) on there saying, "It's like you're slave driving people." Keith Rabois is always on there saying, "No, all the great founders worked their fingers to the bone."

They're talking past each other. First of all, they're talking about two different things. David is talking about employees and a lifestyle business, which is fine. Your number one thing in life, if you're doing that, is not getting wealthy. You have a job, you also have your family, you also have your life.

Keith is talking about the Olympics of startups. He's talking about the person going for the gold medal and trying to build a multi-billion dollar public company. That person has to get everything right. They have to have great judgment. They have to pick the right thing to work on. They have to recruit the right team, and they have to work crazy hard. They're basically engaged in a competitive sprint.

If getting wealthy is your goal, you are going to have to work as hard as you can. But hard work is absolutely no substitute for who you work with and what you work on. What you work on is probably the most important thing.

What you work on and who you work with are more important

Finding Product-Market-Founder Fit to expand on Marc Andreessen's definition, he came up with Product-Market Fit. I will add Product-Market-Founder Fit, which is how well you are personally suited to that business. The combination of that three, that should be your overwhelming goal.

You can save yourself a lot of time if you pick the right area to work in. Picking the right people to work with is the next most important piece. Third comes how hard you work. They're like three legs of a stool; if you shortchange on any one of them, the whole stool's gonna fall down. It's not like you can pick one over the other that easily.

The order of operations when you're building a business, or even building your career, is first figure out, "What should I be doing? What is something where there is a market that is emerging? There's a product that I can build that I'm excited to work on and something where I have specific knowledge and I'm really into it?"

Second, surround yourself with the best people possible, and no matter how high your bar is, raise your bar. You can be working with other people who are great enough. There's someone greater out there to work with, you should go work with them.

I advise a lot of people who are looking at which startup to join in Silicon Valley. I say, "Basically pick the one that's going to have the best alumni network for you in the future." Look at the PayPal mafia. They worked with a bunch of geniuses, so they all got rich. Just try and pick based on the highest intelligence, energy, and integrity people that you can find.

Finally, once you've picked the right thing to work on and the right people to work with, then you work as hard as you can.

Nobody really works 80 hours a week

Now, this is where the mythology gets a little crazy. People who work 80, 120 hour weeks, a lot of that's just status signaling. It's showing off. Nobody really works 80 to 120 hours a week sustained at high output with mental clarity. Your brain breaks down. You just won't have good ideas.

Really, the way people tend to work most effectively, especially in knowledge work, is they sprint as hard as they can while they're working on something, and they're inspired and they're passionate; and then they rest. They take long breaks.

It's more like a lion hunting and much less a marathon runner running. You sprint, then you rest, you re-assess, and then you try again. What you end up doing is you end up building a marathon of sprints.

Inspiration is perishable

Nivi just made the point to me on the side that inspiration is perishable, which is a very good point. When you have your inspiration, do it right then and there. This happens to me a lot with my tweetstorms. I've actually come out with a whole bunch of additional tweetstorms besides the ones that are already out there, but sometimes I just hesitate, or I just pause, and it just dies.

What I've learned is, if I'm inspired to write a blog post or to publish a tweetstorm, I should probably do it right away. Otherwise, it's not going to get out there; I won't come back to it. Inspiration is a beautiful and powerful thing, and when you have it, just seize it.

Impatience with actions, patience with results

People talk about impatience. When do you know to be impatient? When do you know to be patient? My glib tweet on this was, "Impatience with actions and patience with results." I think that's actually a good philosophy for life.

Anything you have to do, just get it done. Why wait? You're not getting any younger. Your life is slipping away. You don't want to spend it waiting in line. You don't want to spend it traveling back and forth. You don't want to spend it doing thing that you know ultimately aren't part of your mission.

When you do them, you want to do them as quickly as you can while you do them well, with your full attention. But then you just have to give up on the results; you have to be patient with the results because you're dealing with complex systems, you're dealing with lots of people.

It takes a long time for markets to adopt products. It takes time for people to get comfortable working with each other. It takes time for great products to emerge as you polish away, polish away, polish away. Impatience with actions, patience with results. As Nivi said, inspiration is perishable. When you have inspiration, act on it right then and there.

If I have a problem that I discover in one of my businesses that needs to be solved, I basically won't sleep until at least the resolution is in motion. This is just a personal failing, but if I'm on the board of a company, I'll call the CEO. If I'm running the company, I'll call my reports. If I am responsible, I'll get on there, right then and there, and solve it.

If I don't solve a problem the moment it happens, or if I don't start moving towards solving it when it happens, I have no peace. I have no rest. I have no happiness until that problem is solved; so solve it as quickly as possible. I literally won't sleep until it's solved. Maybe that's just a personal characteristic, but it's worked out well in business.

36

"Become the best in the world at what you do. Keep redefining what you do until this is true."

Keep redefining what you do until you're the best at what you do

Nivi: We just finished talking about the importance of working hard and valuing your time. Next there's a few tweets on the topic of working for the long term. The first tweet is, "Become the best in the world at what you do. Keep redefining what you do until this is true."

Naval: If you really want to get paid in this world, you want to be number one at whatever it is that you're doing. And it can be niche, that's the point. It can literally be, you're getting paid for just being you.

At this point some of the more successful people in the world are that way. Oprah gets paid for being Oprah. Joe Rogan gets paid for being Joe Rogan. They're being authentic to themselves.

So what this tweet is trying to say simultaneously is that you want to be number one, but you want to keep changing what you do until you're number one. You can't just pick something arbitrary. You can't say, "I'm going to be the fastest runner in the world and now you got to beat Usain Bolt." That's too hard of a problem.

But what you can do is you can keep changing what your objective is until it arrives to your specific knowledge, your skills sets, your position, your capabilities, your location, your interests. And then converges to making you number one.

When you're searching for what to do you actually have two different foci that you have to keep in mind at all points. And one of those is, "I want to be the best at what I do." And a second is, "What I do is flexible so that I am the best at it."

Until you arrive at a comfortable place where like, "Yes this is something I can be amazing at while still being authentic to who I am." And this is not going to be an overnight discovery. It's going to be a long journey but at least you know about how to think about it.

Find founder-product-market fit

The most important thing for a company is to find product-market fit. I would say the most important thing for entrepreneur is to find founder-product-market fit. Where you are naturally inclined to build the right product which has a market and that's a three focus problem. Which is you got to make all three of those work at once.

If you want to be successful in life you just have to get comfortable managing multi-variate problems, multiple objective functions at once. And this is one of those cases where you have to map at least two or three at once.

37

. . . .

"There are no get rich quick schemes. That's just someone else getting rich off you."

. . . .

There are no get rich quick schemes

Nivi: We skipped one tweet because I wanted to cover all of the tweets on the topic of the long term. And the tweet that we skipped was, "There are no get rich quick schemes. That's just someone else getting rich off you."

Naval: This goes back to the world being an efficient place. If there's an easy way to get rich it's already been exploited. And there are a lot of people who will sell you ideas and schemes on how to make money but they're just always selling you some $79.95 course or some audiobook or some seminar .

Which is fine, everyone needs to eat. People need to make a living. They might actually have really good tips but if they're giving you actionable, high quality advice that acknowledges that it's a difficult journey and will take a lot of time, then I think that's realistic.

But, if they're selling you some get rich quick scheme whether it's crypto or whether it's an online business or seminar they're just making money off you. That's their get rich quick scheme. It's not going to necessarily work for you.

We don't have ads because it would ruin our credibility

One of the things about this whole tweetstorm and podcast is that we don't have ads on here. We don't charge for anything. We don't sell anything. Not because I don't want to make more money, it's always nice to make more money, we're doing work here. But, because it would completely destroy the credibility of the enterprise. If I am saying, "Hey I know how to get rich and I'm going to sell that to you." It's ruins it.

When I was young and I was studying up on the topic one of my favorite books on the topic was actually called, How To Get Rich by Felix Dennis, the founder of Maxim Magazine, billionaire who passed away. And he had a lot of crazy stuff in there but he had some really good insights too.

But whenever I read something my him or by the GoDaddy founder, Bob Parsons, or Andrew Carnegie. You read stuff by people who are already very wealthy and they clearly made their wealth in other fields, not by selling the how to get rich line, they have a credibility. You just trust them.

And they're not trying to make money off of you. They are obviously trying to win some status and some ego, right, you always have to have a motivation for doing something. But, at least that is a cleaner reason why they're probably not lying. They're probably not fooling you. They're not snowing you.

Every founder has to lie to every employee

At some level every founder has to lie to every employee of the company that they have. Where they have to convince them that it's better for you to work for me than it is to do what I did and go work for yourself. So I've always had a hard time with that.

Which is why the only honest way, in my companies I've recruited entrepreneurs and I tell them, "You're going to get to be entrepreneurial in this company and the day the you're ready to go start your own next thing I'm going to support you. I'm never going to get in the way of you starting a company. But this can be a good place for you to learn how to build a good team and build a good culture, how to find product-market fit to perfect your skills and meet some amazing people while you figure out exactly what it is you're going to do, because positioning, timing, deliberation, are very important when starting a company."

But what I've never been able to do is look them in the face and say, "You must be at your desk by 8 AM." Because I'm not going to be at my desk by 8 AM, I want my freedom. Or say to them that you're great at being a director today and you'll be a VP tomorrow. Putting them into that cold career path track because I don't believe in it myself.

Anyone giving advice on how to get rich should have made their money elsewhere

If anyone is giving advice on how to get rich and they're also making money off of it, they should have made their money elsewhere. You don't want to learn how to be fit from a fat person. You don't want to learn how to be happy from a depressed person. So, you don't want to learn how to be rich from a poor person but you also don't want to learn how to be rich from somebody who makes their money by telling people how to be rich. It's suspect.

Nivi: Anytime you see somebody who's actually gotten rich following some guru's advice on getting rich, just remember that in any random process, if you run it long enough and if enough people participate in it you will always get every single possible outcome with probability one.

Naval: There's a lot of random error in there and then also, this is why you have to absolutely and completely ignore business journalists and economist academics when they talk about private companies.

I won't even name names but when a famous economist rails on Bitcoin or when a business journalist attacks the latest company that's IPO'ing, it's complete nonsense. Those people have never built anything, they're professional critics. They don't know anything about making money. All they know is how to criticize and get pageviews. And you're literally becoming dumber by reading them. You're burning neurons.

I'll leave you with a quote from the Nassim Taleb that I liked where he said, "If you want to be a philosopher king first become a king then become a philosopher. Not first become a philosopher and then become a king."

Nivi: I'm glad you brought up Taleb because I was going to finish this by saying just remember the title of his first book which is Fooled By Randomness.

Naval: One of the reasons why we're a little vague in this podcast is because we're trying to lay down principles that are timeless as opposed to just giving you the winning lottery ticket numbers from yesterday.

38

"Apply specific knowledge, with leverage, and eventually you will get what you deserve."

On a long enough time scale you will get paid

Nivi: We're still talking about working for the long term, the next tweet on that topic is "Apply specific knowledge with leverage and eventually you will get what you deserve." I would also add to that apply judgment, apply accountability and apply the skill of reading.

Naval: This one is just a glib way of saying that it takes time, even once you have all of these pieces in place, there is an indeterminate amount of time that you're going to have to put in. And if you're counting you'll run out of patience before it actually arrives.

So you just have to make sure that you give these things a proper time, life is long, and Charlie

Munger had some line on this. Somebody asked him about making money and he reinterpreted that and he said what the questioner was actually asking was, "How do I get rich like you but faster before I end up as a really old guy?"

And everybody wants it immediately but the world is an efficient place, immediate doesn't work. You do have to put in the time. You do have to put in the hours and so I think you just have to put yourself in the position with the specific knowledge, with the accountability, with the leverage, with the authentic skill set that you have to be the best in the world at what you do.

And then you have to enjoy it and just keep doing it and keep doing it and keep doing it and don't keep track and don't keep count because if you do you will run out of time. I can look back at my career and the people two decades ago I had identified as brilliant and hardworking but hadn't thought much more about it, they're all successful now, almost without exception.

On a long enough time scale you do get paid but it can easily be 10 or 20 years. Sometimes it's five and if it's five or three and a friend of yours got there it can drive you insane. But, those are exceptions. And for every winner there's multiple failures.

One thing that's important in entrepreneurship is you just have to be right once. You get many, many shots on goal. You can take shot on goal every three to five years, maybe every 10 at the slowest or once every year at the fastest depending upon how you're iterating with startups but you really only have to be right once.

What are you really good at that the market values?

Nivi: My little equation is that your eventual outcome will be equal to something like the distinctiveness of your specific knowledge times how much leverage you can apply to that knowledge times how often your judgment is correct times how singularly accountable you are for the outcome times how much society values what you're doing. And then you compound all of that with how long you can keep doing it and how long you can keep improving it through reading and learning.

Naval: That's actually a really good way to summarize it. It's probably worth even trying to sketch that equation out.

That said, people try to then apply mathematics to what is really philosophy. So I've seen this happen in the past where I say one thing and then I say another thing that seems contradictory if you treat it as a math equation.

But it's obviously in a different context and then people will say, "Well you say that desire is suffering," you know, the Buddhist saying, and then you say, "All greatness comes from suffering. So does that mean all greatness come from desire?" Well this isn't math people, you can't just start carrying variables around and forming absolute logical outputs. You have to know when to apply things.

I think that is very useful to understand but at the same time one can't get too analytical about it. It's what a physicist would call false precision. When you take two made up estimates and you multiply them together and you get four degrees of precision and those decimal points don't actually count. You don't have that data. You don't have that knowledge. In a model, the more estimated variables you have, the greater the error in the model.

So, just adding more and more complexity to your decision making process actually gets you a worse answer. You're better off just picking the single biggest thing or two. For example, what am I really good at according to observation and according to people that I trust, that the market values?

That alone, those two variables alone are probably good enough because if you're good at it you'll keep it up. And if you're good at it you'll develop the judgment. And if you're good at it and you like to do it eventually people will give you the resources and you won't be afraid to take on accountability. So all the other pieces will fall in place.

Product-market fit is inevitable if you're doing something you love to do and the market wants it.

39

....

"When you're finally wealthy, you'll realize that it wasn't what you were seeking in the first place. But that's for another day."

....

When you're wealthy, you'll realize it wasn't what you were seeking

Nivi: The last tweet on the topic of working for the long term is that "When you're finally wealthy, you'll realize it wasn't what you were seeking in the first place. But that's for another day."

Naval: That's a multi-hour topic in of itself. First of all I thought it was a really clever way to end the whole thing because it disarms a whole set of people who say, "What's the point of getting rich?" Because there's a lot of people who just like the status signal, virtue signal, against the idea of wealth creation or making money. So it was just a good way to disarm all of them.

But, it's also true. In that the things that you really want in life, yes money will solve all your money problems but it doesn't get you everywhere.

The first thing you realize when you've made a bunch of money is that you're still the same person. If you're happy, you're happy. If you're unhappy, you're unhappy. If you're calm and fulfilled and peaceful you're still that same person. I know lots of very rich people who are extremely out of shape. I know lots of rich people who have really bad family lives. I know lots of rich people who are internally a mess.

A calm mind, a fit body and a house full of love must be earned

So, I would lean on another tweet that I put out which is actually, when I think back on it, I think it's my favorite tweet of mine. It's not necessarily the most insightful, it's not necessarily the most helpful. It's not even the one I think about the most but when I look at it there's such a certain truth in there that it just resonates. And that is that "A calm mind, a fit body and a house full of love. These things can not be bought. They must be earned."

Even if you have all the money in the world you can't have those three things. Jeff Bezos still has to workout. He still has to work on his marriage or whatever his next relationship is. And his internal mental state is still going to be very much not controlled by external events. It's going to be based on how calm and peaceful he is inside.

So I think those three things, your health, your mental health and your close relationships are things that you have to cultivate and can probably bring you a lot more peace and happiness than any amount of money ever will.

Practical advice for a calmer internal state

So, that's what I meant. Now, how to get there is actually a tweetstorm that I still need to put out. I've been working on it. I have probably a hundred tweets on it. It's just very hard to say anything on the topic without getting attacked from 50 different directions, especially these days on Twitter. So I've been hesitant to do it because I want to target it for a very specific kind of person.

There's a bunch of people who don't believe that working on your internal state is useful. They're too focused on the external. And that's fine, there's nothing wrong with that, they should do that and that's who the how the get rich tweetstorm is for.

There's a bunch of people who believe that the only thing worth working on is complete liberation, like you become the Buddha, and they'll attack anything in the middle as being useless. That's fine too but most people aren't there.

So, what I want to do is to create a tweetstorm that is just very practical advice for everyday people who want to have a calmer internal state. A set of understandings, realizations, half truths and truths, that if you were to imbibe them properly, and again these are just pointers to ideas that you already have and experiences that you already have. That if you keep these top of mind, slowly but steadily it will help you with certain realizations that will lead you to a calmer internal state. That's what I want to work on.

Fitness is another big one, I'm just not the expert there. There are plenty of good people on Twitter that who are better fitness than me.

A lot of divorces happen over money, a lot of battles happen over internal anger

And I think a loving household and relationships actually automatically falls out of the other things. If you have a calm mind and if you've already made money, you should have a good relationship. There's not reason why you shouldn't. A lot of divorces actually happen over money, unfortunately that's just the reality of it, so having money removes that part of it.

A lot of external battles happen because you're internal state is not good. When you're naturally internally peaceful you're going to pick less fights. You're going to be more loving without expecting anything in return and that will take care of things on the external relationship front.

Nivi: So, money solves your money problems. Money buys you freedom in the material world, I think that was a tweet from your cutting room floor, and money lets you not do the things that you don't want to do.

Naval: Yeah to me the ultimate purpose of money so you do not have to be in a specific place at a specific time doing anything you don't want to do.

How to Get Rich
(without getting lucky)

If you enjoyed this book you will probably enjoy our Ancient Wisdom series, available on the link below:

Bite Sized Books publishing
https://bitesizedbook.com

Printed in Great Britain
by Amazon

81096042R00089